MONEY THROUGH THE AGES

MONEY POWER

Jason Cooper

Rourke

Publishing LLC
Vero Beach, Florida 32964

www.rourkepublishing.com

PHOTO CREDITS: © Armentrout; © The Smithsonian Institution National Numismatic Collection; © Lynn M. Stone; © Elwin Trump; © Oscar C. Williams

Cover Photo: *Old coins*

Editor: Frank Sloan

Cover design by Nicola Stratford

Library of Congress Cataloging-in-Publication Data

Cooper, Jason
    Money through the ages / Jason Cooper
      p. cm. — (Money power)
    Includes bibliographical references and index.
    Summary: Discusses ways of paying for goods and services, from the barter system used for hundreds of years to electronic funds transfers that were made possible only recently, and describes the first banks.
    ISBN 1-58952-210-9
    1. Money—History—Juvenile literature. [1. Money—History.] I. Title.

HG221.5 .C663 2002
332.4'9—dc21
                                                     2001048909

Printed in the USA

CG/CG

TABLE OF CONTENTS

THE EARLIEST MONEY

People use money to pay for goods and services. In today's world, money is made of paper or different metals. Each country of the world has its own money. Each piece of paper money or coin has a **value** marked on it. Every $1 bill in the United States is worth just that—1 dollar.

These gold coins were made in the 19th century.

BARTERING

People haven't always used coins and paper bills to pay for things they need. Long ago, people needed little or no money. They made their own shelters and grew their own crops. When they couldn't make something they needed, they traded, or **bartered**, for goods and services. Bartering was the first system of payment. A shoemaker, for example, might have traded a pair of shoes to a farmer for food.

Young people use the bartering system when they trade baseball cards.

TRADING IN THE 1600s

For many hundreds of years, bartering was the only way to exchange goods and services. When large numbers of Europeans began coming to North America in the 1600s, for example, they traded with the Indians who already lived there. The Europeans wanted such things as furs and land. And the Indians wanted goods they couldn't make.

In some countries, people sell or trade food for other items of value.

UNUSUAL MONEY

Any goods traded to North American Indians were a form of money. And among these Indians, people used colorful belts made of shells. These belts were known as **wampum**.

On Yap, an island in the South Pacific Ocean, islanders made stone disks they used as money. These disks weighed 500 pounds (227 kilograms).

The **ancient** Chinese traded seashells for food and clothing. Egyptians used money made of gold rings.

Stone disks were used as money on the island of Yap.

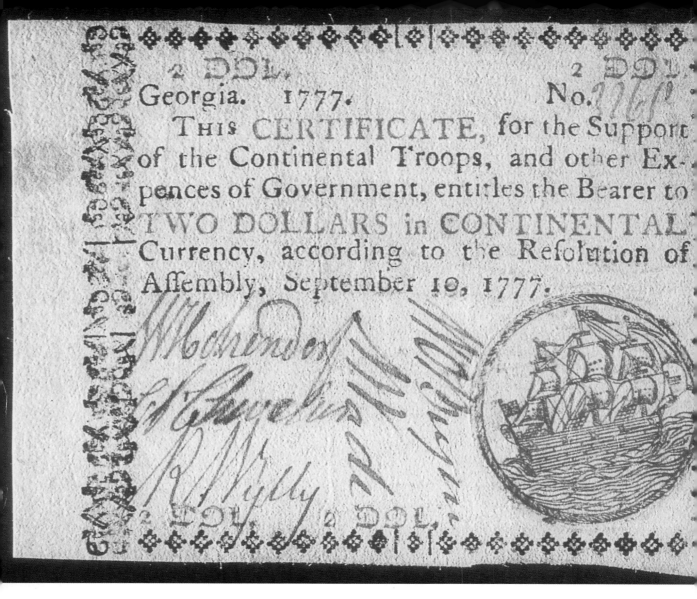

An American $2 certificate issued in Georgia in 1777

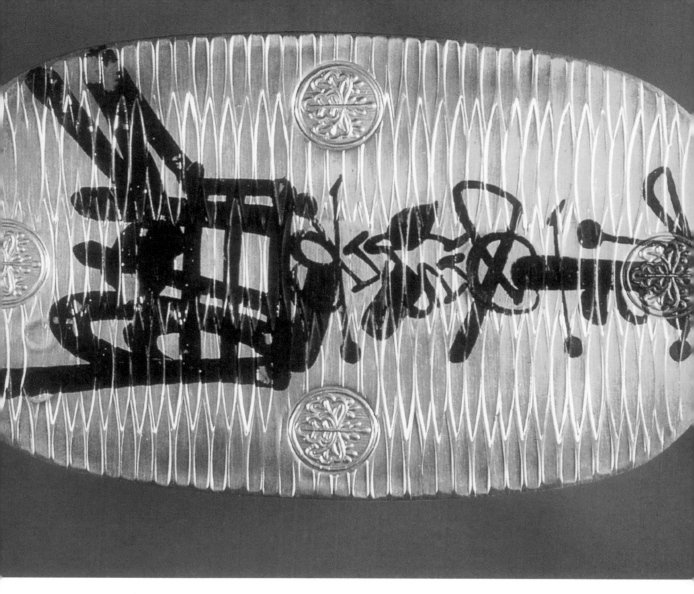

Japanese oban were once used in trade just like money is today.

THE FIRST "REAL" MONEY

"Unusual" money is not easy to use. And the value of traded objects can change greatly in a short time. People began to learn that having a constant, or **standard**, form of money was a good idea.

As long as 2,600 years ago, people in what is now western Turkey began using coins as money. The coins were made of a mixture of silver and gold. They were both strong and valuable. Coins were also used long ago in China and India.

People in Egypt valued gold and made ring money from it.

PAPER MONEY

Even coins, however, could be clumsy because some of them were big. About 1,400 years ago, the Chinese began using paper money. European sailors who traded with the Chinese were amazed. The Europeans did not trust the use of paper money. It was not until the 1600s that people in European countries began using some paper bills.

The Chinese were among the first to use paper money.

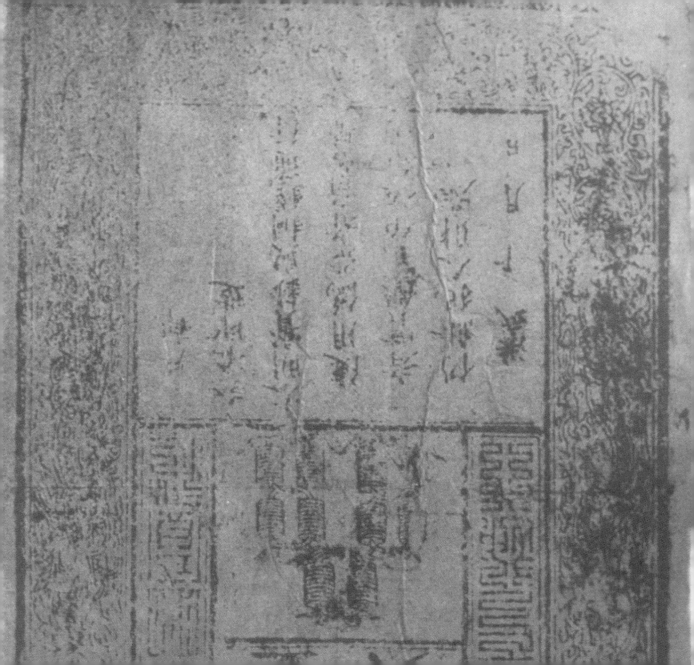

THE VALUE OF GOLD

Long ago gold became popular to make coins. Silver, bronze, and copper were all valuable metals, but gold was rare and beautiful.

Many governments based the value of their money on gold. Governments **guaranteed** the value of their paper money with gold. The widespread use of gold, called the "gold standard," helped make trade between nations easy.

Gold has always been a valued metal. This U.S. coin was made in the 20th century.

ANCIENT BANKS

As ancient people began to save money, they needed a place to put it. They didn't have banks. But they began to store money in **temples**. Temples were holy places. People were not likely to steal from temples.

Temple workers loaned money to needy people. Later, temple workers began to loan money to all kinds of people. The workers earned money called **interest** by charging people to borrow money. Modern banks and people who lend money charge interest, too.

Banks are the most popular place to deposit money.

MONEY TODAY

Money and the ways we use it continue to change. Each year, for example, more and more payments for goods and services are made **electronically**. The actual exchange of paper bills and coins does not happen as often now.

The style of money changes, too. The United States issued paper money with a "new" look in the late 1990s. In Europe, the Euro became the currency shared by several countries in 2002.

GLOSSARY

ancient (AYN shent) — very old

bartered (BAR terd) — traded by exchanging goods or services

electronically (ee lek TRON ik lee) — by means of electricity

guaranteed (gayr un TEED) — to have backed the value of something

interest (IN trest) — money earned by one who loans from one who borrows

standard (STAN durd) — constant

temples (TEM pulz) — holy places

value (VAL yoo) — the worth of something

wampum (WAHM pum) — beads or polished shells used by North American Indians as money

INDEX

Further Reading

Lewis, Brenda R. *Focus on Coins and Currency*. DIANE Publishing, 1999

Websites To Visit

http://www.money.org/
http://www.frbsf.org/currency/index.html
http://www.moneyfactory.com

About The Author

Jason Cooper has written several children's books about a variety of topics for Rourke Publishing, including recent series *China Discovery* and *American Landmarks*. Cooper travels widely to gather information for his books. Two of his favorite travel destinations are Alaska and the Far East.